THE CRE

Enoch's Way of the Yeshurim

By

Dr. S. Asher

CREATORS CALENDAR

PUBLISHED BY KDP 2019
Edited by MJS. LTD

CONTACT – INFO@AHLCglobal.com

PRINTED IN THE UNITED STATES OF AMERICA
ISBN - 9781796833638

Printed in the USA by Amazon Books

About this book

This book is meant to be a real-time guide for those who follow the Creator's original, 1st law path. If you remain unaware of the 1st law of the Everlasting Agreement, please read – *The Land of Meat & Honey,* by Dr. Asher 2011; Since following this calendar means nothing without *Returning* to that original path.

This books main purpose is to keep the *Yehshurim* on time and on target with the Eternal Creator's most ancient and original Memorial and Ingathering harvest day schedule, *as it was in the days of Enoch and Noach;* and as it was later reiterated to Abrahim and to Moshe; and later again taught by the great Essene Master and prophet, Yehshua.

Of equal importance, this calendar system has also been set in time to provide those who follow it with the target dates of future prophetic events which are sure to unfold, and without notice to the rest of the world who continue to follow the Shelanite cults changed times & seasons, and this book proves why they have worked so diligently for thousands of years to that prophesied end.

Yes, there are several versions of this calendar, but none line up and clock so perfectly with both ancient biblical events and future prophesied events, and also in real-time as this system proves to line up.

The Origin Calendar from Enoch

When – Where and Why?

Jeremiah 8:8
"How can you say, 'We are wise, and the law of the Eternal One is with us?' And seeing how the lying pen of the scribes has made it to Lie."

I have been asked many times why there are so many versions of the Creator's "Origin" calendar system – *aka* – *The Enoch calendar,* and unfortunately, there are many more reasons for that than versions of it. Not the least of which is because most who have attempted to understand and apply the data that Enoch received have done so under the incorrect assumption that it can be applied and work correctly on a *spherical* earth model. It cannot.

That said, I will not endeavor in this short guide to elaborate on any of those versions because they are all their if you wish to trudge through the less than academic mayhem.

Does this system still work, is another frequent question. I will say this, that if you do not take at least one entire year, do the necessary sightings, count along to the next quarter marker and live with this or any system that you may currently believe to be "the one", then you will never know the answer to that question. LEARN it and LIVE it is the key to all.

What about the Lunar calendars?

Funny story. Some who know me well, know that some years ago I took a solid two-year stretch to research and live out in my daily life two of the most thriving calendar systems; one alleged to be the Enochian system, the other was the most prevalent Lunar system. I deeply researched all of the biblical and other materials that both sides had to offer, and I can honestly say that on both attempts I completely and utterly proved each one wrong in a matter of two short weeks in one case and only days on the other. I, of course, went back to the gurus of these reemergent systems to ask questions and to provide extensive undeniable proof of wrong understanding. They, of course, took the usual route and just stopped taking my calls and emails.

This all left me once again trying to piece together the original system on my own, of which I was able to get about 75% of the way, but no more. At that time and two years into this quest, a quest I only undertook personally because I knew that the Father would soon, *at that time,* have me begin teaching on certain lost and highly controversial topics, all of which balanced on having the correct days and times; but in truth, the corrected calendar details continued to elude me because I just had not yet taken the time on my long and arduous academic path to also become an expert astronomer. Not that one must be an expert astronomer to *live* with and *use* this corrected system once someone shows it to you, but I believe it would have helped greatly to be one while trying to flush it out. In the end, and after many more years of using yet another, ***nearly*** correct system that eventually proved to clock-out of time in 2017, it appears that my friend, Barry Usher, a Torah teacher was led back into simplicity where all others added only complications and magic and was led to original understanding that uncomplicated everything that I can see. Some parts of the version I was led to use before this remain, while other revelations emerged to correct it all.

In the end, and as I will show herein, this system can be simplified even further to a mere counting of days to the next *quarter*, seasonal change. Even if you live in a cave and only mark the wall with a rock, you will be one of the only people alive celebrating the Creator's Memorial days, on the correct days.

Is that so important?

Isa 1:14 *"your fasting, your Sabbaths, your new moons also, and your feasts my soul hates: you have become troublesome to me; I will no more pardon your sins."*

Amos 5:21 *"I hate! I reject your feasts, and I will not accept your meat-offerings in your assemblies..."*

And as anyone who has studied my work already knows, these are but two of many such replies on the topic of reprobate times and seasons.

For anyone attempting to keep the correct 4-*Renewal Memorial days* which are the fence around the 1st law of the Everlasting Agreement, or the correct "time frame" for their Sabbath's, along with the correct times for our future plantings and harvest festival days, much less all of the end-time prophetic correlations built into this calendar; my suggestion is that everyone become familiar with the required 12 constellations, and not by manmade astrological charts, YouTube videos, photos from NASA or those astrological slide rule inventions and the like. Much better to be able to identify them all with your actual eyes. I have also been shown that it is a good thing to be able to locate Orion's belt. As our 12 related constellations, *one each month*, are said to fall in between the moon and Orion's belt each time, making identification easier.

But again, it really does take some effort to get outside on the specific changeover days/nights to see and learn this stuff in real-time, so you have it for later.

The Quarters, the Shmitah cycle & Moon

Initially, my son and I had a hard time finding Virgo for Asher in the month that we began using this corrected version. FYI: The month of Asher coincides with the Roman calendar in August to Sept 8.

Moon Phase - Additionally, everyone should study this picture of the phases of the moon (below), because one specific phase (per year) is used for identification confirmation *only* on what most people already know as the "solstice-quarter day." (4-times per year)

The moon is used as an *additional* confirmation that you have hit the Quarter, or, (91-day) mark from the last quarter in that year. It is also used to prove *which year* we are in of the 7-year cycle, aka - the Shmitah.

Learning and Seeing the Shapes

Although most pictures of the Constellations vary and seem accurate, for now, it's all we have to get started to learn the basic shapes of the constellations that are listed [in Hebrew] on the following pages. You can correlate their pagan names to the Hebrew names later.

Note: The order of the months was never supposed to be based on the birthing order of the 12 sons of Jacob as most have taught it. The order is based on the MEANINGS of their names. And when one reads the meanings of their Hebrew names from ***Neftali to Zebulun*** it provides a positive message, and in the opposite direction, it becomes a negative message. Barry Usher's corrected, printed calendar has all the names and meanings on each months page. At this time in Feb/2019, I am still trying to get the updated version of that calendar for people to buy and have. For now, I have added those calendar pages to the back of this book for quick reference.

Note: This Origin calendar does NOT end or need to be revised, nor do the days shift or change like all others. Nor do we need to add Leap-Years or a 13th month every 7 years as others do. This calendar just continues to revolve unabated without fail, forever.

Let that be your first proof that this system clocks correctly.

Right to left – Sliver, then ½, then ¾, then full, then ¾, then ½, then sliver – THEN, beginning on the LEFT side we count back to the right again, and so on for 7 years each time = The Shmitah. The guarantee is that you WILL SEE ONE of those moon phases and ONLY one of them on each quarter of a given year.

MEANING, if this year we see the ¾ moon on the 1st Renewal Memorial night, then we will also see that identical moon phase on the rest of that years 3 memorial nights, absolutely! That alone proved to me that *this* calendar is more correct than any other. **It either CLOCKS or it does not.**

Note: Remember, what *we* call a *Renewal Memorial Day*, is also known to everyone else as the Solstice day, although their "solstice" day may NOT be on the same day as they are clocked on *this* Enochian system by the stars and moon. Many may recall that in 2018 their NASA based calculation of the *Equinox day* in March was a whole day off because NASA, in collusion with the Vatican astronomers made a change and admitted to it! *Changing times and seasons...*

So, this added moon phase count not only tells you what YEAR we are in within any 7-year Shmitah cycle but, 49 of those cycles brings us to the Jubilee 50th year.

THE MOON HAS ABSOLUTELY NO OTHER USE IN THIS SYSTEM, AND IN MY MIND IS NOT EVEN TRULY REQUIRED IF YOU KEEP A RELIGIOUS AND ACCURATE 91-DAY COUNT, FOUR TIMES between quarters - THROUGHOUT ALL YEARS. But using the moon does sure make it easier and more foolproof if we lose our place after sleeping too long by the fire in your cave.

Another unexpected surprise was brought to my attention, and something that fits perfectly with everything I have come to know about the Essene's and the prophet Yehshua specifically, which is, that the Essene Grand Master, *Yehshua,* explained things that everyone since has misconstrued to be *the serving and eating of dead fish*, but, in fact, the calendar system that he was teaching to them there in the Galilee.

The Age

The understanding is, that the AGE always influences the people in it. The age of the Bull prior to the age of the fish influenced everyone in it to false idol worship of that sort. Maybe Satan appoints one demon to oversee and directly influence most ages. During the age of the Bull, it appears to have been Moleck. It also might be understood then that the "soul" of Yehshua was sent from the order of the Malek'Zedik to usurp and powerfully influence the age of Pisces and beyond. I say this because, well, history appears to prove that concept. As for what he was teaching on this topic of the calendar, Yehshua, during the beginning years of the age of the fish, was NOT feeding them fish! He was teaching them ABOUT the fish = **Pisces** as being the **AGE** they were in at that time and would remain in for a 2600-year cycle, which only recently, ended in 2017.

Specifically, when they asked him WHEN the prophesied time of trouble would come – *Jacob's trouble* - he tells them to LOOK for the **MAN carrying the WATER!** *Men didn't carry water back then, Women did that!* The man carrying the water is Aquarius -**THE AGE OF!**

So, we have Yehshua explaining that the AGE of Pisces is where they were at that time, and, that it would rule from then, through a 2600-year period, at which time the AGE of the **water-bearer** would come in and rule; and in *that* AGE would come the prophesied events they asked about.

Have you seen me use this picture of the water-bearer in my books and websites for many years now? EVER wonder why I use it? Because the true Hebrew soul can see other Hebrew souls, and Yehshua was Hebrew, NOT Jewish, and most certainly he was not Christian.

AND THEN they asked Yehshua for a sign, and what did he say? - He said that the ONLY *sign* they would get would be the sign of JONAH! WHAT? It is obvious from the texts that they truly did not understand that Jonah's "sign" was a great eclipse that traversed the entire land of Nineveh in his day. Nor was that explained to them. Others tend to believe it was again the sign of the great fish in connection with

Jonah, but that is not correct. Those men were seriously confused by this. But it was not for them to know yet.

AND WHEN did we change from the age of Pisces to Aquarius?
On **August 21st/2017**

AND WHEN did *we* get the prophesied sign of Jonah?
During "The Great American Eclipse"- On Aug 21st/2017!

Keeping things obscured

There is a lot of disinfo out there about when this all-important Aquarius age started. Most say 2012, but that appears to be based on using **Regulus** which, after much research, I have come to believe to be the wrong way to identify it. Some sources also tend to say that an **AGE** is around 2170 years, which again appears inconsistent with most ancient writings. Even the Jewish, Babylonian Talmud, among other ancient texts, show an "*age*" to last 2600 years. Since more sources tend to show and agree that "an age" is 2600-years, and that *Aquarius* [Passed-Over] from *Pisces* in Aug of 2017; and, having that in connection with it the sign of Jonah (The Great American Eclipse) which created darkness over the entire land for 3 hours *as it was written!* I'm going with August 2017.

Ancient correlations

2600 years ago from Aug 21st/2017 to 583 BCE is interesting, because 3-years later, specifically counted by Ezekiel *while using the original Creator calendar* as being (3)-PASS-OVERS later, the land was invaded, and Solomon's temple was destroyed in 586 BCE.

Ezekiel appears to have used two separate calendar systems while in captivity. First, he used the Babylonian civil calendar to keep a record of their captivity. In that calendar, the years began in ***Tishri*** and is the same Babylonian system Jews use today. The second calendar he used was known as "the sacred system", and given that this calendar started and ended on a PASS-OVER day, this most certainly had to have been the original *Creator given Enochian* system. To know why we must venture further back in time. In more ancient times than those *Hebrews and Jews,* the original PASS-OVER day was understood to be the day we now call the "Intercalary" day at the head of each year – [Check for the *Neftali* calendar on page 96].

This is but one of 4 days that are "watched" as PASS-OVER points from *either* one year to the next as we see Ezekiel doing here, *or,* from seasonal quarter to the next quarter – [Intercalary days]. It was the later, Babylonian influenced Jews who moved its "name" to the end of the 14th day, which is known in their culture to be the 15th day – *Babylonian style.* As per the Genesis account and as reiterated to Moshe upon receiving the law of the Sabbath, a **Day** begins at SUN-UP! A day does NOT begin at night! How can DAY begin at NIGHT? That is entirely Babylon-Speak.

Yes, they later intermingled Babylonian paganism with the original meaning of the first Exodus, which was and is meant to be understood as a "Memorial" and not some relocation of a calendar [Pass-Over] event day. It was and is meant to be understood as the [Day of Mannah-bread]; which has always been that months day of Re-planting of crops from previous years. The Creator's elohim Yehovah used that specific 15th day on that month to emulate the reestablishment and Re-planting of the Eternal One's people to a new location.

Meant to be a double Memorial Day from that 15th day forward! First, of the original Memorial Day of planting crops in the new year, then, of freedom from their Egyptian slavery in that year. Moreover, as time progressed and through the Eternal One's prophets this 15th day also became the memorial for looking ahead in anticipation for the prophesied, Greater Exodus to come!

THIS IS NOT to say that there are now 4 Passover celebration days during all years! The 4 *Yehshurun* Renewal Memorials come a day later after the intercalary days hit.

VERY IMPORTANT:

In this calendar system, we separate the idea that there are 4 Intercalary days; there are Days of the month = 30, *and,* there are days of the week = 7. This makes up a total of 360 days + 4 Intercalary days.

Intercalary Days:

The Intercalary days are very misunderstood, but should be understood as [marker points] in the system that create PASS-OVER points to ***both,*** the next new YEAR as we see only in the month of Neftali, ***or,*** within any year to the next Quarter or Season in that year.

Most people have been taught to know these points as Solstice days. As you will see reiterated in this guide several times, these Intercalary days are (91-days) apart. And yes, of course, each Intercalary day is ALSO understood and seen as Day-3 in all months, which then gives the system a total of 364 days in each year.

Week Days:

The Weekdays are shown at the top row of the calendar month; the days of the month are obvious and run 1 through 30. [Refer to calendar pages].

Day 4 is a very specific marker day and derived directly from the Genesis creation day 4 account. On that day we see that the Creator literally started the clock, which is why each YEAR and each MONTH rotates around and begins again on THAT day, and THAT day ONLY! The 4th day was and remains a memorial to the initial start day and countdown to the end of this creation event.

Days of the Month:

As stated, the days of each month run 1 through 30, there is no trick to this part. You will see on the calendar pages that the other memorial days and prophetic event days can be seen to fall on one of those 30 days in the month, BUT ALSO, the important *Ingathering* memorials are always found to fall on the 15th day of that month, which, if you slide back up to the top of the calendar you will always find that day to fall on the all-important 4th day of the week. You will also see that no memorial or prophetic days fall on any Sabbaths.

The following lays out the timing:

- *Intercalary day = Weekday 3 = Pass-Over day.*
- Weekday 4 = 1st Memorial = 1st day of 1st month.
- *Intercalary day = Weekday 3 = Pass-Over day.*
- Weekday 4 = 2nd Memorial = 1st day of 4th month.
- *Intercalary day = Weekday 3 = Pass-Over day.*
- Weekday 4 = 3rd Memorial = 1st day of 7th month.
- *Intercalary day = Weekday 3 = Pass-Over day.*
- Weekday 4 = 4th Memorial = 1st day of 10th month.

After the 4th Renewal Memorial, we then count the last (91-days) back around to the next New Year again, and it all starts over without changes.

Important note: If you must correlate these days each year with your pagan Roman calendar, remember that their calendar MOVES AHEAD one day each year. **Example** - This year, 2019, the 1st Renewal Memorial falls on their Roman 13th day of March. Next year it will be the 14th, and so on.

Word of advice. I realize in this current world we are forced to use their manipulated, pagan systems, but the two systems MUST be kept separate. Like Ezekiel, we are forced to use one for daily life here in greater Egypt, and the other for our spiritual life. But do NOT make the Creator's system subservient.

Ezekiel tracking events using the Sacred System

- 588 BCE – Nebu'Khan'nezzar attacks Jerusalem in the tenth month - (Ezek. 24:1) in January.
- 587 BCE – Siege is on.
- 586 BCE – Nebu'Khan'nezzar's nineteenth year - Nisan (March/April) - Temple destroyed in month of *Ab* (August)
- 585 BCE – Ezekiel's 1st Passover after destruction of Solomon's Capital city – [By invasion]. By that time Ezekiel has been in Babylonian hands for 13 years.
- 584 BCE – Ezekiel counts 2nd Passover since temple destroyed.
- 583 BCE – Ezekiel counts 3rd Passover since temple destroyed - Ezekiel's 15th year in captivity.
- 583 BCE - Signifies a 2600-year PASSING OVER from the age of the Bull (Aaron's golden calf and Ba'al worship) into the AGE of the Fish – Pisces for 2600-years until August-21st/2017.

August – Month of Asher 21st 2017 Passes Over to the Age of Aquarius.

FOLLOWING ARE THE CORRECTED MONTHS w/corresponding constellations to become familiar with:

NAFTALI = ARIES = MARCH:

- (Intercalary day = Passover – no sign in the sky at all)
- Next day is 4th day of week and 1st day of new year
- First Renewal Memorial - (look for sign that night)
- Day to Re-plant seeds – 15th day of Month.
- 15th day is the day of leaving Egypt & Re-Planting.
- Looking for the Greater Exodus!
- **Neftali is ruled by the White horse of Revelation.**

YISSICHAR = TAURUS = APRIL

SHIMEON = GEMINI = MAY:

- 15th day is 60-day Harvest gathering day- ***Shavu'ot***.
- The Intercalary day is at the end **after** the 30th day
- No sign in the sky)

YOSEF = CANCER = JUNE:

- 4th day = 1st day of next quarter = 91-days from Neftali-1
- Change to summer.

- *Second Renewal Memorial.*
- **Shimeon is ruled by the Red Horse of Revelation**

YEHUDAH = LEO = JULY:

ASHER = VIRGO = AUGUST:

- 8th day was 2017 Sign of Jonah
- 15th day is Daniel's 1260th day

LEVI = LIBRA = SEPTEMBER:

- 3rd day is also 1275th day of Daniel
- 4th day = 1st day of next quarter – Change to Fall
- *Third Renewal Memorial*
- 15th day is agricultural Ingathering day
- 15th day is also Daniel's 1290th day
- 17th day Noah's Ark rested just before Sabbath
- **Levi is Ruled by the Black horse of Revelation**

DAN = SCORPIO = OCT:

- The 30th day of Dan is Daniel's 1335th day
- <u>It is also a Sabbath day</u> & <u>in the winter</u>

GAD = SAGITTARIUS = NOV:

BENYAMIN = CAPRICORN = DEC:

- 3rd day is Intercalary day
- 4th day = 1st day of next quarter - winter

- *Fourth Renewal Memorial*
- **Benyamin is Ruled by the pale horse of Revelation.**

REUBEN = AQUARIUS = JAN:

- 10th day – End 40 days-Sends Raven & Dove
- 17th day – Dove sent the second time
- 24th day – Dove does not return; waters abated

ZEBULUN = PISCES = FEB:

- Season to change to spring after the 30th day
- 1st month - Neftali begins the next New Year!

They changed times and seasons, and it was prophesied that they would do it!

Jub 2:9-10 *"And the Eternal One appointed the sun to be a Great sign on the earth for days and for Sabbaths and for months, and for festivals and for years and for Sabbaths of years and for Jubilees and for all Seasons of the Years."*

Jub 6:32-33 *"And command the children of Jacob that they observe the years according to this reckoning and not leave out any day nor disturb any appointed times. They are memorials from the* ***first*** *to the* ***second****, and from the second to the* ***third****, and from the third to the* ***fourth****."* [Easy - 1-2-3-4 & NOT 7!]

Jub 6:38 *"They will not make the year 364 only, and for this reason, they will go wrong as to the months and seasons and sabbaths and festivals..."*

By adding the word "and" in Genesis 1:14-19 it virtually forces the reader to assume that the luminary being referred to just prior to it MUST be the MOON! Nothing could be further from reality.

The Hebrew word for moon

Yareach isn't found within a thousand miles of this Genesis text. The reality is that the Sun is the

GREATER light and the STARS are the *lesser light* being spoken of here, and in Enoch, and in other texts which they clearly redacted from the cannon, and from the minds of the those it was meant for.

You may recall my teaching on this topic of the moon-*Yareach*. That the later Torah "Correctors" changed the word *Chodesh* to mean - New Moon.

Chodesh means MONTH or NEW MONTH. Some that apologize for the texts and the Shelanite redactors say that they merely confused the word *Chodesh* with the word *Chadash. Problem is,* they have very different and specific meanings. *Yareach*, as I mentioned, is the word for moon and *Chadash* means [New]. Together, of course, that phrase – [Yareach Chadash] would mean

New moon, however, you will NOT find that phrase in the entire Tanak regardless of how hard you look for it.

Adding additional injury, the *Correctors* also changed and retaught the word *Yareach-moon* with the like word – *Yarach*, which means month – *i.e. complete month cycle.* This is where all the moon calendar worshipers went wrong in believing that the so-called NEW MOON was the real beginning point of all new months.

As I have previously shown in my books, the original 4 holy Renewal Memorials as they were written and known to be held in heaven, were also the true memorial days observed by Adam, to Methuselah to Enoch, Noach and his family along with Abrahim and company after them. They are also the original 1st law memorial days that were part of the "reiteration" instructions that Moshe originally received on Mt. Horeb for all the sons of Jacob to learn and do afterward. Yet, as we know, most rejected for ANOTHER law from ANOTHER entity on ANOTHER mountain – ***Sinai.*** Most "expert theologians" have completely misunderstood what these four holy memorial convocations are, not fully grasping just how horrifically the texts have been manipulated – "corrected", to redirect and control people. Thus, the following texts show the FIRST day of the solar month to be that special Memorial Day - ***in its specific quarter months****. i.e. the 1st, 4th, 7th & 10th* months on the Enochian calendar – Sacred Calendar as already shown.

Enoch 74:12 *"And the sun and the stars bring in all the years exactly so that they do NOT advance or delay their position by one day, forever; but complete the years with perfect justice in 364 days."*

Enoch 82:6-7 *"One in the first portal and one in the third, and one in the fourth and one in the sixth, and the year is completed in 360 and 4 days. Their accounting is perfect and the reckoning of them is exact for the luminaries, months, and festivals, and years and days..."*

After the Babylonian captivity, they had already long abandoned His Sacred Origin Calendar system for their Babylonian-style Moon calendar, then, later to their own version, the 'Talmudic calendar.' The Talmudic Calendar is a lunisolar calendar using *Tishri-years*, observed since the Late Antiquity {AD 300-700}.

Additionally, it is based on *Nisan-years*, which began in the pre-biblical Babylonian era {c. 2000 BC}, with the *Tishri-years* formed in the time of King David {c. 1000 BC}. The full version of this lunisolar system was formed during the time of the writing of Talmud {c. AD 280-600}, of which is generally attributed to Rabbi Hillel II.

Thus, we can clearly see the prophecy within both Jubilees, to Noah, the prophets and other books as coming true in spades concerning those who would use the moon exclusively, thereby dislodging all of the Eternal Creator's original *days, dates,* and *times* for His everlasting Renewal Memorials. All which revolve around His *1st Law of the Everlasting Agreement!*

The four horses

Enoch 82:9-13 *"And these are the orders of the stars which are set in their places, and in their seasons and the festivals in their months. And these are the names of those who lead them, and who watch over the entrance of their appointed times and in their order, in their seasons, in their months and periods of dominion, and in their positions."*

Their four leaders who divide the four parts of the year enter first:

- *The four riders which are the Intercalary days,* they are leaders which capture the four parts of the year.
- The 12 Leaders - *Constellations/tribes of Jacob* - of the orders who divide the months;
- And these heads are over thousands and between Leader and Leader, each behind a station, but their leaders make the division…"

Obviously, these "divisions" are known as the intercalary days – PASS-OVER points.

Psa 104:19 *"You have made the month to mark the seasons; the sun knows it's time for setting."*

Equal parts day & night:

Many people searching out this calendar system continue in error not knowing the 1st law, it's boundaries and meaning. Additionally, most of them continue to maintain and incorrectly believe that the specific geography of Jerusalem alone is to be the single point on earth where the annual, calculated *Passing-Over* point of March 16th – *the day of equal day and night* each year (for that region) should be marked from.

Of course, they show some Prophetic texts that *appear* to uphold the overarching importance of Jerusalem – Tzion, as being the only place on earth that the Eternal One and His servant Yehovah are viewing or maintaining watch over, etc. I tend to differ in opinion on this point based on the plethora of textual proofs which I have presented so many times now through many years which point to the scribal changes, along with my own personal and direct experience.

Specifically, scribal changes [by the correctors] that are always created to point back to them as being the sole keepers of the truth, and sole authority over all of its meaning.

The fact is, that we have been and remain spread throughout the world by the design of the Eternal

One and His legions. And I have shown through the prophecy of the ***Greater Exodus*** and the ***Beacon-Seed*** books that we are meant to find the original path and return to it regardless of location. And in order to return to it more perfectly, we will also require the original calendar system. Another obvious point being, that while we are so spread out, we cannot be certain to receive any verified celestial sighting data from Jerusalem each year. Thus, we are left to find this data point of the intercalary day and then the day AFTER – being the 1st day of the new year on our own, wherever we may be. Which of course may be a slightly different timing than others throughout the world.

Now, where others see this to be a flaw in the system, I see a greater perfection from the Eternal One. Where their idea gets everyone clocked on a single day for each festival and regardless of location, giving homage to "some god" using their own ways and means all at the same time. I see that being so spread across the world to be creating a human wave of worship that slowly spreads across the entire surface and ongoing, while everyone doing this is worshipping the Eternal One in His way, and as He gave it!

How can we keep or apply that static time of the 16th of March when it only occurs in Jerusalem and its surrounding areas? Surely it will not be the 16th where you and many others may be? Is the answer that we all move to Israel now? NO! Absolutely not, because that then negates the entirety of the Greater Exodus in its day. Should we just abandon the entire calendar and the four most holy Renewal convocations and ingathering days until after the Greater Exodus relocation program? And that forces us to believe that the Greater Exodus, and "the land" that we will all be traveling to, to in fact be Jerusalem-Canaan! Many have made quite excellent arguments using those same prophetic texts to prove that the "land" in that day, will not be Israel/Canaan at all.

Regardless, my life mission has been to seek my Creator and DO His will, now, not later. I have yet to hear one single Prophet tell me to just wait until some later date, or that I had to be in one specific place on earth. And yes, I have heard the argument that if everyone uses that March 16th date each year now, that this will still create that worship-wave I speak of because everyone's March 16th day will begin at various times, etc. And maybe that's good enough. But the texts that override it all for me say to use the SUN and the STARS wherever I am, to find WHERE and WHEN I am, and NOT THE MOON exclusively! So, I am instructing that everyone become acquainted with the 12 specific constellations and seek them out each month in the sky over your head with your actual eyeballs, then YOU will see when a past month's "sign" disappears, and also see when the new "sign" appears on that 1st night of that 1st day. And YOU will know "when" you are, regardless of "where" you are. Yes, others may be around who can, using mass communications, for now, tell everyone when that day is supposed to be close and the approximate dates of that New Year's Day, etc., but, when we cannot communicate, then what? And more importantly, whether they be Jew, Messianic Jew, Messianic Christian, Catholic or Muslim, they all use the moon as the basis of their systems, and they are all 100% wrong in doing so. *Just as it was prophesied to happen.*

Believe me, if the Greater Exodus occurs in our lifetime, He will send a Malakim to line out the Yeshurim with all the specifics just like it happened with Moshe. Do you believe that Moshe did not know his calendars, the stars or time? Of course, he was a Prince of Egypt, schooled and mastered in all of the most important disciplines. Problem was, his culture, being Egyptian to that point did not provide him with the understanding of *this* ancient, *Sacred Calendar* system. *Meaning*, that Moshe, already being a master of astronomy, the Malakim of the Eternal Creator did not need to do more than to readjust Moshe's start point, calendar reference.

As proof, we see only the following, minimal instruction to Moshe which continues to go on totally misunderstood to this day.

Exodus 12:1-2. *"And the Malakim of the Eternal One said to Moses and Aaron in the land of Egypt, saying, this month will be to you the beginning of months. It will be the first month of the year to you."*

See? So don't stress it! If for some unknown reason we are off a bit on that day, it will be readjusted.

As we have seen, 360 & 4 Days completes one rotation of the year, and Enoch continues to show that there are 30 days in each month, along with the added, 4 intercalary days – One day added at the end of each season in that PASS-OVER month to divide the four Riders/seasons. I already explained this, but this point always seems to throw people. What confuses people is that these *intercalary days* "appear" to make those four months have 31 days in them, but technically this is NOT the case. [Return to pg. 21 again for this data]

Additionally, you will see once you have one of these calendars in hand, that each intercalary day ends or "creates" the "Passing-Over" point at the end of months 3, 6, 9 and 12. THEN! The NEXT day AFTER each of those *intercalary* days is our 4 Renewal Memorial days which fall on the 1st day of that new month/season. Which as we already know begins on the **1st day of the 1st month – 1st day of the 4th month- 1st day of the 7th month and the 1st day of the 10th month.**

As for the Equal Day & Equal Night scenario being one and the same as the Vernal Equinox?

Enoch is explicit in saying that we begin the new year AFTER the intercalary day, which will be the day/night when the new constellation (sign) moves in.

Of course, we will see it best at night, and the best times to view these signs does vary and is yet another part of this system that must be learned. Will that DAY also begin and end with equal parts light and on the exact EAST – WEST track as the shadow on the ground via a Sundial should also prove? Yes, all things being equal and depending on where you are the sun during that single day should prove to be equally as accurate as the sign of Neftali revealing itself on that same night; and, additionally, as should the moon phase for that year also reveal itself correctly for verification.

THAT understood, if we have no way to accurately measure the sun on that day, two out of three – *the star sign and the moon,* should be more than enough. ESPECIALLY if you kept an accurate (91-day) count from the previous year.

Back to Equal parts light

Enoch clearly states that the night hours and day hours will be equal. Problem is, and most likely the main contributor to why the former Enochian calendar system version that many were following veered off course after a few years, is because we were using the "officially stated" Vernal Equinox *exclusively* as the start point, and NOT the star sign. And that, in most cases, has been dictated to us by NASA. So, when I say we use the stars, I mean PHYSICALLY LOOKING!

Do NOT utilize ANY of this worlds star maps, star calculators or other instruments or projections to find the alleged Vernal Equinox or the 12 constellations, they are ALL WRONG! (All use this systems algorithm)

They are ALL made for this worlds skewed versions of systems which men have created, and they will NOT fit within the observation of this Sacred

Enochian calendar system. I CANNOT stress this point enough. USE YOUR EYES! LEARN TO SEE!

A Single Point in Time

The problem that led us off course while using the calculated and stated Vernal Equinox as the head of our year was not taking into consideration that the Vernal Equinox is measured at a specific place and point in time which is *directly over the equator*. Making matters worse, is, that calculation is based on a spherical earth model. So, possibly even the Jerusalem based March 16th date would have kept everyone closer to the correct count over using the official Equinox.

Another issue that we have run into while attempting to sight the stars and moon is our Chem-Trailed skies, where even in the most historically clear areas such as in the many Western States, there are now far too many Chem-covered nights that will definitely obscure the signs from being seen on their specific days. Much less find the exact night that rings in the new year. Truthfully, it was not until we began actively sighting the constellations each month that we began noticing how most nights were clear here, but amazingly within a day or two before the month changed, the skies were chemtrail to no end. And the night skies obliterated leaving us to guess afterward.

Knowing how epically important it is for the people of the Eternal One to know and follow the true times and seasons; while being acutely aware of how hard and long the dark side has worked to obscure the availability of His calendar system which now in the end times has been recovered, I personally have no doubt that this is at least a part why the Chemtrail operations were commenced. Created to obscure our last-days ability to read the signposts.

Truly, we will all have to seek the Eternal One and ask for those times to be clear to us.

One additional point concerning the idea of using that March/16th date from Jerusalem each year for a worldwide start date for this calendar. I ask this question, *'are you also going to keep Israel's Sabbath day as well?'* Because their Saturday is NOT going to be the same day in America, South America, Hawaii, etc.

As I stated, this system is created to work (in worship) as a human wave from end to end and back again through the years.

Enoch 72:31-33 *"And on that day the sun rises from that portal, and sets in the west, and returns to the east, and rises in the third portal for 31 mornings, and sets in the west of the heaven. On that day the night decreases and amounts to nine parts, and the day to nine parts and the night is equal to the day, and the year is exactly as to its days – 360 and 4."*

Growth Pains

9/11/18 – Was the Intercalary day/night PASSING-OVER from Asher/Virgo to Levi/Libra and the sign of Asher/Virgo should have completely disappeared from where we saw it in the night sky previously. And to prove it all, the moon (see below) should have been 3/4 LEFT of Center in the picture. Which means we are in Year-3 of the Seven-year count. Right? However, that is not how we all looked for it at that time.

Following the moon Phases in the Quarters

The MOON appears to move in BOTH directions, and originally it was explained to me that the moon rises in the East for 6 months of the year, and then from the west for the last 6 months, but this is not something that I have been able to observe or confirm. I also cannot find anyone else who explains such a phenomenon other than to say that because the moon does shift far north and or south during its travels, that sometimes it *appears* to rise from the Western sky.

However, I will also note here that virtually everyone who explains these things is basing their understanding on a Spherical, spinning earth model.

As pointed out previously, while we track the moon phase for a given year to identify our 4 quarters every 91-days, as well as where we are in the 7-year counting towards the 49-years to the next 50th year Jubilee, we also use the single moon phase (for the year we are in) to track and confirm our correct position in that calendar year by SEEING the specific moon phase that corresponds to that years, New-Years-day/night.

Again, if we watch the moon phases from right to left, we see seven phases.

And, in each year, ONE, and only ONE of these phases will be evident and displayed on those 4 Intercalary days/night for the changing of the seasons – 4 times in the year. New year's - 2018 was moon-phase picture #1 above. Problem was, the Jewish tradition taught everyone to look for the *lighted portion* of these phases, but that is not the truth. The moon phase that we actually witnessed with our eyes on the 1st Memorial Day/night of 2018 was picture #1 above, a lighted ¼ sliver. While still having some confusion, everyone looked for the ¾ lighted moon phase at that time, which made us think that we were in the wrong year because we were looking for the ¾ *lighted* phase.

At that time the updated calendar information was coming into me rather slowly, but we did finally get caught up days later to correct the error.

Now for another possible important correlation back to the changing of the Age too – **Aquarius**.

If the age shifted from Pisces to Aquarius with the sign of Jonah traversing the entire land if the USA in darkness on August 21st, 2017, as we believe, then my tendency is also to believe that the final 7 years began after that, and must be in conjunction with the 7 moon phases.

Meaning, the moon phase chart shows us that in 2017 - 2018 we were in year 1 of the 7-year Shmitah counting. From 7 years of light to 7 years of darkness as represented by how we track these moon phases. *By their darkened side, not by the lighted section during THIS 7-year cycle.* Just that we were initially looking at the moon phases incorrectly as already explained; we were to seek out the DARK ¾ side of the moon phase in the pictures below, on the far-right side.

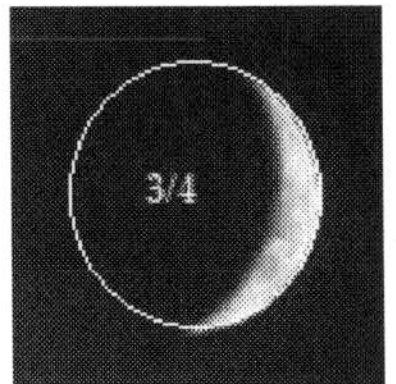

This would put us in year 1 of the 7 moon cycles. In 2019 we should be sighting for the ½ DARK side moon phase, or picture number two from the right, above.

This then puts us in year 2 of the 7-year count. If I am correct about this, we are in the first 3.5 years of Jacob's trouble, or Tribulation.

So, there's more to the story with sighting the 7 moon phases in each month and for the years. This is something else which has been hidden from us.

Dark vs. Light

Now that we know how to read the moon phases for counting the 7-year Shmitah and the yearly seasonal quarters, and as previously posited, them teaching everyone to sight only the *lighted* side of the moon was a partial lie to keep everyone off track, seeing that if you only track and discern the LIGHTED side of the moon phases, then you are only tracking and discerning ONE-HALF of the ordinances!

Meaning, depending on the 7-year cycle we are in – [*i.e. following the moon from right to left or from left to right or for 7-years*], we are supposed to be tracking a different side of the moon depending on which direction we are tracking in. Why? Because, in relation to the sun, the moon has shifted or flipped sides.

EXAMPLE – Most may be inclined to believe that the Shelanite cult does not have their count correct based on their highly corrupted Babylonian calendar, *or do they?* The prophecy is that they will change ***appointed times and seasons,*** but it does not specify for whom they will change. Certainly, they have kept the real count to themselves in order to hold all the power over the masses. I do believe, however, when the Eternal One clearly stated that He hates THEIR Sabbath's and THEIR new moons, THEIR festivals and THEIR many prayers, that He has allowed THEIR counting to coincide with the time of THEIR destruction. *Meaning,* they may have appeared to change their calendar outwardly, while inwardly they have always remained true to the original Enochian system which they call – *The Sacred Calendar.* As I showed earlier, they were using it in Babylon alongside the Babylonian system as we saw with Ezekiel. But, after leaving Babylon the only calendars they used ***outwardly*** were Babylonian based, just as their modern calendar remains, and is synonymous with the Roman calendar which is also Babylonian based.

And remember this, it was the Jewish orthodoxy who told the world that the "Jubilee event" would occur on this date in 2016-5777. Why does the world take their word for it when they lied about virtually everything else?

So, for this example, we will use their timing of the last **Shmitah** year which was alleged to have kicked off their 49th year to the 50th year Jubilee in 2016. And understand, I am now seeing this as a ruse, an early Jubilee timing meant to throw the world off. I am also NOT saying that their individual 7-year counts are off, I doubt they are, which is why I believe we can use this timing.

Their last "manipulated" Shmitah year cycle count had them tracking and discerning their ***Dark sliver portion*** of the moon phase during that 7-year cycle from 2008 - **NOT the lighted side!** This was meant to show that they were coming OUT of the darkness and INTO the light, beginning in that next 50th year! Get it?

And where have we been hearing that same line in government circles – ***Coming out of the darkness, into***

the light? Problem is, if that were true, then we would have seen the LIGHTED ¾ phase in 2018 and not the lighted sliver as we witnessed.

Additionally – That for this to be true in 2016 for them, then our Enochian calendar would have had to SHOW us the ¾ LIGHTED side moon phase on all of our intercalary days in 2017-2018, but that was NOT the case! On that day we saw the Darkened ¾ moon phase as I already depicted!

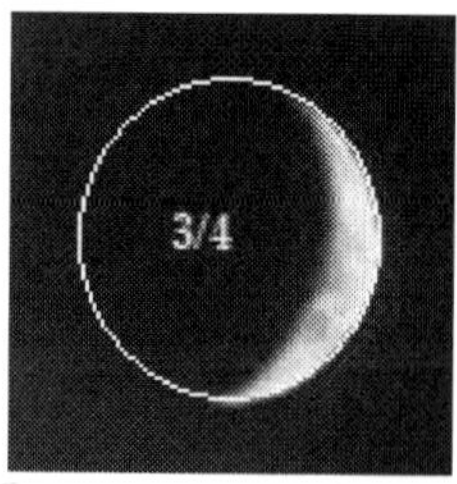

Which means, either this calendar is wrong, or the Shelanite-Judahites are lying to everyone again? I bet you know which way I'm leaning on that one!

Why would they lie about that? Why of course, ***to keep us in the dark about the light!*** *Meaning*, they tell the world that the Great Shmitah-50th-Jubilee came and went and that now we have entered a cycle of Light/Plenty/Security, etc.; but that has not been the visible case around this world, has it? It has seemed more and more like darkness over the past few years for sure, and more than any other time I can recollect. WHY? To keep the chattel unaware of what is coming, **so that no one repents like Nineveh**.

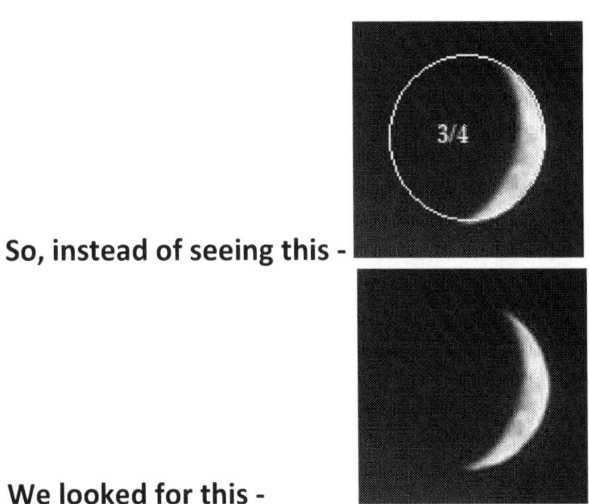

So, instead of seeing this -

We looked for this -

Most believe that the number 70 is a prophetic number.

Daniel spoke of 70, *sevens* that must be fulfilled in order *for redemption to come*. The "alleged" 70th Jubilee Shmitah that occurred in 2016 was believed by all Jews to be extra significant! It is widely believed by all Jews and most Christians who follow their lead, that this past 2016 Jubilee Shmitah will mark the beginning of a prophetic series of events that could ultimately culminate seven years later.

In the years 5774 (2013/14) - 5775 (2014/15) … They also appeared quite proud of the fact that they, the world, would have four lunar eclipses during this time frame. A smart person might recall and consider that the last time a lunar eclipse marked an event for Jerusalem, the country, and specifically that city, it got sacked over a period of 3.5 years, and finally leveled by Nebu'Khan'nezzar, as I described earlier. Again, why did we take their word for all this? Keepers of the law and the count?

Counting Sabbatical Years – Shmitah

So, by sighting the moon phase in 2018 correctly, the calendar is now proven to be accurate. The other way we identified its accuracy was by how the next constellation (Levi-Libra) came in on time on Sept/11/2018. (Note: 3 sevens – Year 5777 = Begins Finality!)

So, in THIS 7-Year Shmitah count, we will continue tracking ONLY the DARK side phases of the moon from right to left. And when we change over after the 7 years are done, to work our way back from left to right at that time, we will then be watching the moons LIGHTED side for the phases. *It would appear that we are currently in year two - 2019,*

Have we forgotten what Josef said to Pharaoh?

Gen 41:25 *"Then Joseph said to Pharaoh, "The dreams of Pharaoh are one; God has revealed to Pharaoh what he is about to do. 26 The seven good cows are seven years,* [Shmitah] *and the seven good ears are seven years; the dreams are one.* "

28 "It is as I told Pharaoh; God has shown to Pharaoh what he is about to do. 29 There will come seven years of great plenty [Light] *throughout all the land of Egypt, 30 but after them, there will arise seven years of famine,* [Dark] *and all the plenty will be forgotten in the land of Egypt."*

32 "And the doubling of Pharaoh's dream means that the thing is fixed by God, and God will shortly bring it about."

Job 9:9 *"He is the Maker of the Bear and Orion, of the Pleiades and the constellations of the south."*

Job 38:31 *"Can you bind the chains of the Pleiades, or loose the cords of Orion?"*

Job 38:32 *"Can you bring forth the constellations in their seasons or lead out the Bear and her cubs?"*

Amos 5:8 *"He who made the Pleiades and Orion, who turns darkness into dawn and darkens day into night, who summons the waters of the sea and pours them over the face of the earth, Aheeyeh is His name."*

So, to simplify this, the moon is a (marker), and used to track a different ANGLE of the moon every 7 years! One seven-year segment of *lighted moon* portion, and the next seven-year segment of the *darkened portion.*

Used ONLY to verify what you should already know via your accurate 91-day count to the next seasonal change-day, or by your accurate sighting of the new constellation coming in on that 91st night. Or both!

The Path of Destruction – The Umbra!

Rev 12:1-2 *"And a great sign was seen in the heavens, a woman having been clothed with the sun, and the moon was underneath her feet, and on her head a crown of twelve stars;*

2 and having a babe in the womb, she cries, being in labor, and having been distressed to bear.

3 And another sign was seen in the heavens, and, behold, a great red dragon having seven heads and ten horns! And on his heads were seven diadems, 4 and his tail drew the third part of the stars of the heaven, and he throws them to the earth. And the dragon stood before the woman being about to bear so that when she bears he might devour her child. 5 And she bore a son, a male, who is going to shepherd all the nations with an iron staff. And her child was caught away to God, and to His throne.

Rev 12:6 *"And the woman fled into the wilderness, where she had a place, it having been prepared from God, that there they might nourish her a thousand two hundred and sixty days."*

On August 21st/2017 – The day of the Great American Eclipse, just as the previous Revelation passages depict would happen as the sign of Jonah – The Sun was still ruling, but the people could still also see the stars and the moon at the same time. And the sign of Jonah passed-over the whole land for 3 hours of darkness.

In all likelihood, that day started the countdown to the first 3.5 years as prophesied. BUT, if you go back and read all of the 7 warnings that I received and published, you will see they show that only the last, *1-year period,* of the final 3.5-year period as being the worst part of it.

(If those days were not shortened?) Did we not also see this same timing with the final year of total destruction by Nebu'Khan'nezzar's army over Jerusalem as I cited earlier, and as codified by Ezekiel?

The four *original* warnings I presented, initially are based on the original prophecy of Jonah, *which was the sign of his coming to Nineveh,* their coming destruction, and the future fulfillment of it here. Which would later be further recognized prophetically as the sign of Jonah through the prophet Yehshua, and to be played out at some later date - The great eclipse of August 21st/2017. As you may have come to know from reading my earlier works, that all of these things are like the crops – Cyclical! Whether it is the parable of the wheat and tares proving the cycling of souls in and out or the destruction of nations, it can always be found to be of a cyclical nature.

What happened to His people before, will happen again! When continues to elude us.

Some may recall that I strongly suggested no one go out to watch or *give homage* to the so-called *Great American Eclipse* of 2017. I warned to ignore it, even on TV or the internet. At that time, being worried that some may have Loht's wife influence still, I went so far as to advise people to quarantine themselves wherever they were, homes or offices, etc. It must have sounded alarmist, even superstitious of me, but knowing the many details of so many relevant things I felt motivated to make the advisory.

Well, it has now been brought to my attention that more might be understood from that event and meant to tie into events of the not so distant future and the warnings I received about an invasion from the south.

My original impetus for this warning came in part from the knowledge that many ancient peoples, and even a few remote tribes today, still believe that their people have been *turned* in some way, both mentally and spiritually after watching such an event, even possessed. And these reports are well spread out from ancient times and still persist, so it's impossible to believe they are all imagination. So, given the times we appear to be living in, better safe than sorry was my thinking.

The Shadow Knows and Marks them!

The Moon's umbral shadow is about 166 miles across as it covers the Earth. The eclipse *totality* lasted about 10 minutes (over you) during the Great American Eclipse in 2017, with the shadow sweeping the full width of the country, west-to-east, lasting three hours. Only observers within the *umbra* see the total solar eclipse. Observers outside of that, or the – *penumbra*, are affected less and see a partial solar eclipse. Judging from the lack of change in the light coming through our windows here so far north, no darkness fell on us.

Personally, whether it sounds superstitious or not, I believe that those who knew it to be the sign of Jonah, whether they believed it important, or true, or not, and paid homage to the rare sign as it occurred anyway, may also be adversely affected by what comes next. ***Meaning***, those it touched may have been marked along with the multitudes who should have known better.

Think of all the *area* of the ground that came fully within the path of the umbra/darkness from west to east on that day. Now, think of it as the Prophesied *Path of Destruction to come.* And think of all those who willingly paid homage to it on that day, to have been ***marked*** on that day on their foreheads and right hands. And for all those *Yehshurim* who did not heed that warning to remain sequestered and ignore the sign, may your flight from that area and surrounding areas when that day comes, *not be in the winter or on the Sabbath day*. Which brings me to Daniel's 1335-day as it falls on this corrected Creator's Origin calendar.

As it was in the Days of Noach! – Noach's event timing correlates perfectly in this calendar!

It suffices to say, that this clue as given by Yehshua directly above clearly proves that all future prophecy which extended through and beyond his time, must be in line with everything that occurred in the Days of Noah!

Is that difficult to surmise and understand now?

Gen 7:6 "**And Noah was six hundred years old** when the flood of waters was upon the earth.

Gen 7:7 "And Noah went in, and his sons, and his wife, and his sons' wives with him, into the ark, because of the waters of the flood.

Gen 7:8 "~~Of clean beasts, and of beasts that are not clean.~~ And of fowls, and of every animal that creeps upon the earth, 9 "There existed two and two with Noah in the ark, the male and the female, as the Eternal One commanded Noah. (Strikethrough texts were Priestly addition.)

Gen 7:10 "And it came to pass after seven days, that the waters of the flood were upon the earth.

Gen 7:11 "In the 600th year of Noah's life, in the 2nd month, the 17th day of the month, *that day* were all the fountains of the great deep broken up, and the windows of heaven were opened." – **[THIS WAS Yissachar 17 – Day AFTER Shabat!]**

Gen 7:12 "And the rain would be on the earth 40-days and 40-nights - **[Until the 26th day of Shimeon]**

Gen 7:13 "In that same day Noah, Shem, Ham, and Japheth, and Noah's wife, and the three wives of his sons entered into the ark; 14 "They, and every beast after his kind, and all the cattle after their kind, and every creeping thing that creeps on the earth after his kind, and every fowl after his kind, every bird of every sort. **[Still on the 17th day of the 2nd month – Yissachar]**

Gen 7:15 "And they went with Noah into the ark, *two by two* of all flesh, wherein exists the living soul. **[Only those with Souls!]**

Gen 7:16 "male and female of all flesh as the Eternal One commanded him: and the mighty one Yehovah shut them in. **[Still 17th day of Yissachar]**

Gen 7:17 "And the flood was 40-days upon the earth, the waters increased and lifted the ark, and it was lifted up above the earth. **[Lifted off on Shimeon 26!]**

Gen 7:18 "And the waters prevailed, and increased greatly upon the earth, and the ark went over the face of the waters. **[Sailing away on Shimeon 26]**

Gen 7:19 "And the waters prevailed greatly upon the earth; and all the high hills that were under the whole heaven were covered. [20] "15-cubits upward did the waters prevail, and the mountains were covered. [21] And all flesh died that moved upon the earth, both of fowl, and of cattle, and of beast, and of every creeping thing that creeps on the earth, and every man; [22] all in whose nostrils was breath that was on the dry land, died. [23] And every living substance was destroyed which was upon the face of the ground, both man, and cattle, and the creeping things, and the fowl of the heaven; and they were destroyed from the earth: and Noah only remained alive, and they that were with him in the ark.

Gen 7:24 "And the waters prevailed upon the earth 150-days."

Technically the 40-day count is not the most important portion of these texts. It is the 150-day count beginning on the 17th day of that 2nd month – *Yissachar*.

150-days from Yissachar 17 brings us directly to Levi 14, which is the day directly before the first crops ingathering day of Levi 15. That is NOT coincidental. Nor will it coincide like this on any other calendar system.

Gen 8:1 "And God remembered Noah, and every living thing, and all the cattle that was with him in the ark: and God made a wind to pass over the earth, and the waters were depleted;

Gen 8:2 "The fountains of the deep and the windows of heaven were stopped, and the rain from heaven was restrained; 3 And the waters returned from off the earth continually: and after the end of the 150-days the waters were diminishing. **[Levi 14 – Day before LAST Ingathering Day/15th]**

Gen 8:4 "And **the ark rested** in the 7th-month, on the 17th-day of the month, upon the mountains of Ararat. **[Again, this occurred the day before the Sabbath!]**

Gen 8:5 "And the waters decreased continually until the 10th - month: In the 10th-month, on the 1st-day of the month, were the tops of the mountains seen. **[Benyamin 1=*Renewal Memorial Day!* Leaving Winter!]**

NOTE: It should be understood here that the Ark was closed, and all animals remained in hibernation for the winter months. And, that this is a picture of the *Yeshurun* being hidden, provided for and protected throughout the greatest catastrophe. It should also be noted that there was still nothing growing outside that could sustain the animals.

Now watch as this progresses.

Gen 8:6 "And it came to pass at the end of 40-days, Noah opened the window of the ark which he had made: **[Reuben 10 – the day AFTER the Sabbath!]**

7 "And he sent out a raven which went out and all around until the waters were dried up from off the earth; 8 he also sent out a dove to see if the waters were abated from off the face of the ground; 9 but the dove found no rest for the sole of her foot, and she returned to him into the ark, for the waters remained on

the face of the whole earth: He took her, and pulled her into the ark –[***This all took place in one day on Reuben 10***] -[10] and Noah remained another seven days.- [***7 days after Reuben-10 = Reuben 17 = day AFTER the Sabbath again – Noah re-launches Dove.***]
[11] Again, he sent out the dove from the ark; [***On Reuben 17 AFTER Sabbath again***] - And the dove came into him in the evening; [***on the 17***th] and in her mouth was an olive leaf: So, Noah knew that the waters were receding from off the earth".

Gen 8:12 "And he stayed yet another 7-days; [***Reuben 24 and AFTER yet another Sabbath day***] - and sent forth the dove; which returned not again unto him any more."

NOTE: Realize, that the ark and the other animals are still closed up and in hibernation.

Gen 8:13 "And it came to pass in the 601st-year, in the 1st month, on the 1st-day of the month, the waters were dried up from off the earth: and Noah removed the covering of the ark, and looked, and saw that the face of the ground was dry. [***This falls directly on the next year's 1***st ***Renewal Memorial Day!***]

Gen 8:14 "And in the 2nd-month, on the 27th - day of the month, was the earth dried."

Gen 8:15 "And God spoke to Noah, saying, [16] "Go from the ark, you, and your wife, and sons, and sons' wives and [17] bring out with you every living soul with you of all flesh, of fowl, and of cattle, and of every creeping thing that creeps upon the earth; that they may breed abundantly in the earth, and be fruitful, and multiply upon the earth. [18] And Noah went out, and his sons, and his wife, and his sons' wives with him: [19] “Every beast, every creeping thing, and every fowl, and all that creeps upon the earth, after their kinds, went out from the ark.”

Exactly 1 year and 10 days! And that 27th day falls on the 4th day of the week which is the calendars original Genesis, creation day! It all clocks!

UNDERSTAND!

This flood story is found within all of this worlds ancient cultures and writings. Ever wonder why?
Because THIS story is meant to be reiterated and understood in its original context – *As it was in the days of Noah* - so that the souls of this place will SEE it as more than a fairytale, re-learn its true meaning, and make the changes required – [**Returning to the Everlasting Agreement**] - and then be counted as one of the Up-Right if you or your progeny are alive during the next, *Days of Noach.*

Do NOT be fooled – Noach and his family and extended family members, sons wives, were SAVED because they were absolutely obedient with what they were told and given. They were NOT saved by grace!

Exodus – Counting the days

I prove the falsity of the entire animal killing, sacrificing and flesh consumption narrative of the *added* Shelanite Passover more deeply in my books, so I only want to touch on a portion here that I believe has to do directly with this calendar and their changing of the times in their attempt to keep the *Yehshurim* out of balance and away from knowing it.

Exo 12:18 "In the 1st-month, on the 14th-day of the month, at *evening* you will eat unleavened bread, until the twenty-first day of the month, at evening."

As I pointed out in previous sections, the most ancient accounts and understanding in many languages and cultures concerning the PASSING-OVER event was solely based on the original Enochian calendar reckoning and had nothing to do with Egypt or Hebrew slaves. In Hebrew, it is very easy to change the number FOUR, as we see above in Exo:12, to FourTeen - [אַרְבַּע-עֶשְׂרֵה] = *Arba'esrei.* And, although the English translators like to use *Fourteenth*, that variation will not translate directly back into the Hebrew that way.

I have shown a myriad of Hebrew text redactions and changes in my teachings which are not nearly all that exist, but enough to prove a long-standing criminal conspiracy of immeasurable proportions being consistently perpetrated on the souls of this world over thousands of years. So, I do not believe it to be a reach if we decide to understand that here again, in the previous Exodus passage, that they shifted the FOURTH DAY - *Renewal Memorial* down to the 15th day to create a more specific memorial marking the end of slavery. (Remember, the Shelanite cult believe that a DAY begins at NIGHT), so, *their* Passover begins at Sundown on the 14th, which is technically the next day - *which is also the 3rd day of the week if one slides down from week one to week two.*

Slide down from week 1 day 4 which equals the *Passover* END point, to 14th / 15th day which is also day 3 to 4 in *that* week, again.

This is NOT to say that the mighty one of the Eternal – *Yehovah* – did not instruct Moshe and company to "add" that 15th day as the 7th and final minor memorial event to be held as such, *in remembrance*, continually, he did, and those texts do seem to prove that.

However, much later, the newly formed and segregated Shelanite cult who took the name of Judah – (See Asher Codex 2012), began augmenting all of the 7 memorial days *in their Babylonian image*. They did it then, and have continued unabated driving falsehoods from their Mystery Babylon Citadel – *Jerusalem!*

In all of that, and because all of the Babylonian holy days occurred on the 15th - *Mid-Moon* point of certain months, this Exodus 15th day remembrance memorial of the **Hebrews** fit nicely for them, and simple to usurp.

Then is keeping the 15th Passover evil?

Well, what does make it wrong and evil is their continued hiding *of* the 1st law of the *Everlasting Agreement* and mingling the pagan practices of sacrificing and consuming animals in with the Righteous 1st law of Peace.

That Memorial Day was created as another memorial event to commemorate an end to slavery and a look forward to the coming, 2nd and Greater Exodus, and as such it is fine today if you wish to do this.

Again! Historically the NAME or original understanding of the PASSING-OVER event day falls on the 3rd day of each Quarter in this calendar, and known as the *Intercalary* or PASS-OVER day, and has no ritualistic connection to the later, Creator added 15th day, Exodus Remembrance Memorial Day.

Counting Days & Months

This calendar depicts TWO "day" count methods that run parallel, but also need to be understood and viewed as distinct at the same time. THIS IS VERY important to understand.

Hebrew's do NOT count 1 through 30, although 1 through 30 is depicted on these calendars for ease of understanding.

Hebrew's count in SEVENS - 1,2,3,4,5,6,7 – etc. This will become clearer when you see the calendar pages in this book. With all that, and concerning the previous Exodus texts, I only want to show you another aspect of how they changed things and used this calendar to make those early changes.

Exo 13:4 *"Today, in the month of Abib – [March], you are going out."* - [On the 15th day]

Note: Day of Bread, means Day of Mannah!

Exo 13:6 *"Seven days you will eat Mannah, and on the seventh day keep a memorial to the Eternal.* [See the Asher Codex book for the original translation of the entire "unleavened bread feast" understanding.]

In my Asher Codex, I show that there was *never* any actual prohibition for *Leaven* before or after the Exodus. There was never, and will never be any prohibition for consuming leaven. They only had to change the *meaning* of one single word in those texts in order to change the way generations believed and celebrated that 15th-day memorial. They misguided generations just enough by using another *meaning* of the Hebrew word - "Saba."

This was yet another of the many text manipulations in Exodus 12 and 13 that allowed the rabbis to teach it their way for all generations going forward. Other more direct textual additions in Exodus 12 revolved around the pagan practices of killing, burning and consuming animals ritualistically.

Saba - This word has three different meanings depending on the context in which the word is used. I explained in the Asher Codex that in ***this*** context it could only have been used to mean "Perpetually".

Meaning, you will eat only bread, ***not animals,*** forever. And, the bread being referred to is not manmade bread since we know that what they carried away with them only lasted days or a couple of weeks at most, and they had no ability to grow more wheat or barley. So, the bread that is being referred to was *Mannah* which was about to come their way.

שבע= Saba, or Shaba or Sheba – All different words with the exact same spelling:

1. Saba = Satisfied, as in *extensive length of days*, by extension, *indefinite days*.
2. Shaba = Swearing as in crying out or in prayer.
3. Sheba = Numerical Seven

Another point of contention in that same verse 13:6 is this - *'and on the seventh day keep a memorial to the Eternal.'*

Which should have been rendered better to reflect it as their first instruction towards keeping the 7th day Sabbath. Rather than to morph it as some new special *feast week* which they later made it into. The corrected Ex 13:6 verse, if we are to keep the whole line in context with itself, should read like this:

Exo 13:6 *"On day seven you will eat unleavened bread – [Mannah] - And on day seven keep a memorial to The Eternal."*

Exo 15:23 *"And they came to Marah. And they were not able to drink water from Marah, it was bitter. Therefore, one called its name Marah.* 26 *And He said, if you carefully listen to the voice of Aheeyeh your Creator, and do what is right in His eyes, and you give ear to His Law and keep all His statutes, I will not put on you all the diseases which I have put on Egypt; for I am Yehovah your healer."* (Note: ***Healer*** is the wrong translation of (רפאים)=Raphaim. And although Raphaim has a bad connotation being the descendants of the Nephilim and Anakim; tall, mighty, giant people; I believe it is used here, in description form of Yehovah as being their Mighty one in a way they understood, but not "healer.")

I provided the previous texts to once again prove and reiterate to everyone that by this point in their short journey, in chapter 15 of Exodus, that they were already provided a complete Law to obey. As I have explained in my books and teachings, Moshe received the original 1st law of the *Everlasting Agreement* on Mt. Horeb, and *that* is the law they were murmuring against by this time in their journey. No other law was given to them or referred to at all by this point, not even the Sabbath with any real detail yet.

Exo 16:1 "And they pulled up stakes from Elim. And all the congregation of the sons of Jacob came into the Wilderness of Tsin, which is between Elim and Sinai, on the 15th day of the 2nd month after their going out from the land of Egypt."

The 15th day of the 2nd Month "Yissachar" falls on the 6th day of the week, and has them stopping before the Sabbath! Try making that line up on any other calendar! As we go, when using this corrected calendar we see that whether it be Noach or Moshe, the Eternal's Malakim always has them stopping before or after the Sabbath, giving them time to set up and get situated to whatever comes next. Again, this will not line up consistently correctly on any other calendar system. Which is how I know the Noah timeline dates will be used again in the future prophesied events.

So, the Malakim of *Aheeyeh* has them stopping, setting up camp on the 6th day of that week (Friday the 15th) just in time to make them keep a Sabbath. Again, this is just prior to receiving the Sabbath and Mannah instructions.

NOTE: Exo 16:2 *"And all the congregation of the sons of Jacob murmured against Moses and against Aaron in the wilderness,* [3] *saying to them; 'It would have been better to die by the hand of God in the land of Egypt while sitting by the Meat-pots, and eating our bread to satisfaction. But you brought us out into this wilderness to kill all of us with hunger."*

(Meanwhile many thousands of head of cattle stood by them, untouched?)

Just reiterating yet again how the story shows that their main gripe against Moshe centered around their new prohibition of killing and eating the animals.

Exo 16:4 *"And the Malakim said to Moses, Behold* ***I AM****! - [Aheeyeh] 'Bread will rain from the heavens for you. And the people will go out and gather enough for a day, in its day, so that I may test them, whether they will walk in this Law or not."*

This is still within day 15 of Yissachar – **Friday.** And as it is written in this chapter – Tomorrow will be a Sabbath to you! - During the DAY! **NOT Friday night!**

I will also point out that this Friday, 6th day timing for receiving the Mannah, which to them in that wilderness was akin to an Ark of safety and survival, is the exact same timing we saw with *Aheeyeh* resting Noach's ark on Mt. Ararat on a Friday, on Levi-17, just prior to a Sabbath then as well. This is no coincidence. Nor do these Sabbath days of rest line up with all the stories and the dates given in those stories the same way on any other Jewish or Roman calendar, nor any other ancient calendar system.

AS IT WAS IN THE DAYS OF NOACH!

I want to reiterate this point specifically concerning the Memorial dates (Refer to calendar pages) as I have presented them herein and in my Podcast teaching in the Members area of the AHLCglobal.com site.

These "days" are very specifically related and highly important to those who follow the original, 1st law path, namely, the *Yehshurim*. The event days absolutely must be watched and waited for with the expectation of ***provisions*** and ***protections*** for some, and utter destruction for most. If you are still following the Christian Judaic or Muslim cults who use the many manmade calendar variations, while having knowledge of this long-ignored calendar system, then you will surely be caught within those events unaware.

Yehshua – aka – Jesus, very clearly prophesied about the coming – DAYS OF NOAH; but outside of the specific days in their specific months as depicted in this origin calendar, his statements on the subject remain misunderstood and provide no aid to those they were intended for. Many people over near countless generations have attempted to correlate the ancient – *Days of Noah* with their current events, but what good is that? Believing you are seeing the same overall situation or events building up to, yet another similar event crescendo is not an accurate way to discern or predict any of it, and to date, they have all been wrong.

So, then, prophets and *profiteers* throughout time and today read the texts and having some idea of what those end-days are *supposed* to look like still haven't helped, because having some nebulous idea of what these future events look like is only one small part of this equation. You NEED the accurate and specific dates!

- In which year will it come again?
- What season will it come in?
- On what day might it come?

Wouldn't having some specific knowledge concerning those questions be helpful to us in paring down the actual time of that next end, event? Shouldn't we also think further outside the box and consider more deeply why and how the forces of evil have been changing the times and the seasons for a millennium? Whether it's Chem-trailed, obscured sky's so we cannot accurately determine this calendar, or false astrological data throwing us off further, or sphere earth vs. flat earth obfuscation, or the arrival of Santa Clause, it is all devised in part to keep the Living-Souled people out of the correct understanding of the times and seasons, and thus, out of synch with the Eternal Creator. With us also being caught off guard and out of position with everyone else in those end-time events.

NOW, think back again to how the Malakim of the Eternal One dealt with Moshe when he *re-clocked* Moshe back on track with the correct calendar. Even Moshe to that point was using a manmade calendar system that was never aligned with the Creator.

So then, obviously having this calendar is more than just about keeping track of holiday events!

If they have been working tirelessly to stop us from knowing the times & seasons. Don't you think that we ought to take the times & seasons seriously so that we can also know the future? Rather than be caught up in that future with the rest.

Who are you? Who will you be?

I have made mention of what may be misconstrued as different *classes* of people. I have mentioned the titles of the *Yehshurun*, and also of the *Elect*.

Unfortunately, if you have not yet read any of my other works you do not know these terms, their definitions or where they came from, so this short segment is for you.

Yehshurun, or collectively-Yehshurim: (Yehshu-reem)

- Root – Asher & Yasher = Upright/Righteous
- Spoken from the Eternal Creator to Enoch
- Those who obey and follow the 1st law
- Those who are NOT under or judged by the 2nd law

The Elect

- All others who are not yet considered Yehshurim
- They have been and are covered by the Elect one
- Covered by him as viable souls until the GE
- GE = The Greater Exodus
- Not only those in Christianity but all people
- Not labeled Elect because of their righteousness
- Governed & judged by the 2nd law

Following is a literal translation of Enoch chapter 50 to prove the existence and nature of both peoples.

Enoch 50: 50:1-4 "[1]*In those days a change will take place for the "Righteous ones*" [Yehshurun] *and the "Elect"* [Those who follow the Elect one], *and the light of days will come upon them. Glory and honor will turn to the Righteous ones* [2]*on that day of affliction on which evil has been stored up against the sinners. The Righteous ones will be victorious in the name of the Eternal One of Spirits, and He will cause the others* [the elect and others] *to witness this so that they might return, and leave the works of their hands*- [false doctrines]. [3]*They* [the elect ones] *have no honor through the Name of the Eternal One, yet, through his name* [the Elect one], *they will be saved, and the Eternal One will have compassion on them, for His compassion is great!* [4]*And he* - [the Elect one] - *does right also in his judgment. In the presence of his glory* - [the Elect one], *wrongdoing will not maintain itself. At his judgment* - [the Elect one] *the unchanging people will perish before him."* **(Hebrew University Oxford 1821 translation). My additions in [brackets] for text clarity and emphasis.**

Translation: This is by far one of the most important ancient texts that anyone can understand correctly.

- *A change will take place on Yehshurim & Elect?*

I believe this is the same change that Yehshua spoke of and showed his followers. From this physical body back to our original light-body.

- *Righteous ones [Yehshurim] will be victorious in the name of the Eternal One of Souls?*

Here is the first proof that two camps exist. And as I have explained in my Asher Codex, this is also where all of Christianity, Islam, and Judaism have gone wrong.

The *Righteous ones* are considered Righteous because they are the few who *found* and *keep* the 1st law of the Eternal One. They are victorious in all things spiritual, and here specifically during the end times events because they had **previously** shown themselves to be obedient to His law of the ***Everlasting Agreement***. Over which this calendar system presides.

- *"and He will cause the others* [the elect and others] *to witness this so that they might return, and leave the works of their hands*- [false doctrines], and be saved.

Here is it clear again the identity of "the others" being the "Elect." Who are shown the error of their ways for repentance. (To **Return** = Teshuvah). It is also clear that prior to their repentance and RETURN to the original 1st law that they "Have no honor" through the Name of the Eternal One. But, are *saved* anyway by the *Elect one* who they always followed, albeit incorrectly and without knowledge.

Last but surely not least is the Elect one!

- [4]*And he* [the Elect one] *does right also in his judgment. In the presence of his glory* - [the Elect one], *wrongdoing will not maintain itself. At his judgment* - [the Elect one] *the unchanging people will perish before him."*

I have admitted my opinion many times that the job description of the *Elect one* as outlined throughout the book of Enoch, does sound eerily identical to that of the prophet Yehshua, *aka,* Jesus. Additionally, I am on record saying that literally no one inside Christianity or Judaism has a clue about their own relationship to this Elect one, or to the Eternal Father.

Enoch was clearly shown that the Elect one's job was to be the *firewall*, the *covering agent,* standing between all the decent but misguided souls and the Eternal Father. That because of their unclean and unrighteous state of being, the Holy Father had to be firewalled from them all, but NOT disconnected from them as it says the fallen ones were. That if not for this one time *sacrifice of position* by the Elect one, all of those souls would have been cut loose like the fallen angels and lost forever.

Outside of the very few who "Teshuvah=Return" to His original law and path in all generations – separating the Wheat from Tares, none could be saved.

The Past will Prove the Future

AS IN THE DAYS.... The 17th day appears to be the day to watch for!

I reiterate:

Gen 7:10 "And it came to pass after seven days, that the waters of the flood were upon the earth.

Gen 7:11 "In the six hundredth year of Noah's life, in the 2nd month, the 17th day of the month, *that day* were all the fountains of the great deep broken up, and the windows of heaven were opened. – [Yissachar 17 – Day AFTER Shabat!]

Gen 7:12 "And the rain would be on the earth 40-days and 40-nights - [Until 26th day of Shimeon – the 3rd month]

Gen 7:13 "In that same day Noah, Shem, Ham, and Japheth, and Noah's wife, and the three wives of his sons entered into the ark; 14 "They, and every beast after its kind, and all the cattle after their kind, and every creeping thing that creeps on the earth after his kind, and every fowl after his kind, every bird of every sort. [So, we are still on the 17th day of the 2nd month – Yissachar]

Gen 7:15 "And they went with Noah into the ark, two by two of all flesh who had the breath of life.

[Meaning – ALL WHO HAD SOULS!] Those who perished in the flood were *unredeemable souled people* and possibly at that time even a certain percentage of Soulless humanoid entities.

Gen 7:16 "And they went in male and female of all flesh, as the Eternal One commanded him: and the mighty one Yehovah shut them in. [Still 17th day of Yissachar]

Gen 7:17 "And the flood was 40-days upon the earth, and the waters increased, baring up the ark, and it was lifted up above the earth. [Lifted off on Shimeon 26!]

Gen 7:18 "And the waters prevailed, and were increased greatly upon the earth; and the ark went over the face of the waters." [Sailing away on Shimeon 26]

So you see, ALLOT happened on that single 17th day of that 2nd month. THIS was "the day" that the proverbial *shite* hit the fan for the known world. And this is the single day that was noted by the mighty one Yehovah as being the single time when the true intention of a "man" - Noah, "men, women & children", were seen as being completely convinced of the Eternal One's *character, law,* and *word*, and proven by their full obedience! All others were in total rebellion.

They were told the water would be coming, NOT HOW, and they eventually, WHILE WATCHING, saw it begin and then made the necessary move of sequestering themselves INSIDE the ark. Just as the Eternal One – AHEEYEH - has told us by His prophets to have ourselves sequestered for a short time in our dwellings until the judgments PASS-OVER! And when did this happen for Noach and family? Right after that years PASS-OVER event, in the first month. BUT…If you are in the wrong calendar and wrong month, you and yours are swimming!

It would appear to me, given all the data and corrected dates, that we should be looking towards this 17th day on THIS calendar system each year for the kick-off event. Yes, the enemy has us believing we are seeing the end days, all day, every day, of every year, but their attempts are both limited in scope, and in the end, futile; Because the mighty one of this place, when he finally lets loose, I am certain that he will begin letting loose on that exact 17th day. And exactly as we see in those previous Genesis texts. Those who KNOW and keep track of this system and live within the Eternal One's 1st law will have a short time to get themselves sequestered to ride out those indignations.

WHAT IS A SHORT TIME?

Good question. And a relative one at that. And the length of our sequester may even have its "time" *Augmented* so that what we perceive as a day or one week, may actually be one year or a hair over one year as we clearly see depicted within the entirety of Noach's adventure - *One year and 10 days*.

We also see this one-year span with Moshe, although most never saw it. I go into that in one of the chapters in my Asher Codex book. That the span of time between Moshe receiving the 1st law on Mt. Horeb and finally leading them out of Egypt was one year. As it was in the days of Noach!

Note: 1yr and 10-days = 370 days = 3+7+0=**10**

At the top of the tree of life, the Sephiroth, the ***infinite*** Ein Sof is AHEEYEH! The 10th position!

AS IT WAS IN THE DAYS OF NOACH

I don't believe anything out of the mouth of Yehshua to have been wasted breath. This phrase was and remains utterly important to those who can SEE. These days matter!

Back to the Pass-Over ritual question

The 1st month, 14th day, Passover event was as we see, shifted from the 3rd day to the end of the 14th day, making it by Jewish/Babylonian law the 15th day. But the real ***Exodus*** memorial as given was on that 15th day.

As already shown, they later shifted its meaning and ritual behaviors. Thus, when we keep it, it should be understood that it is not the same event *spiritually* as the commanded 4-Renewal Memorial event days which are known to be kept in heaven, perpetually.

Jub 6:25-32 *"And on the **head of the first month** he was told to make for himself an ark; and on the day the earth became dry, he opened it and saw the earth. And on the **head of the fourth month,** the mouths of the depths of the abysses beneath were closed. And on the **head of the seventh** month, all the mouths of the abysses of the earth were opened, and the waters began to descend into them. And on the **head of the tenth** month, the tops of the [lower] mountains were seen, and Noah was glad. And on this account **The Eternal ordained these feasts for a memorial, forever** - Thus are they ordained. And AHEEYEH placed them on the heavenly tables, **each had thirteen weeks*** [91-days]; *from one to another passed their memorial, **from the first** to **the second**, and from the second to **the third**, and from the third to **the fourth**. And all the days of the commandment will be **fifty-two** weeks of days, and **these will make the entire year complete**. Thus, it is*

> *written and ordained on the heavenly tables, and there is* ***no neglecting this commandment*** *for a single year, or from year to year. And command the children of Jacob that they observe the years* ***according to this reckoning*** *– 364 days, these will constitute a complete year;* ***and they will not disturb its time from its days and from its memorials****; for everything will become dislodged in them according to their ideas; thus, they will not leave out any day nor disturb any memorial."*

Do you SEE the absolute importance of these 4 Memorial days? And don't mistake the wording: …*And on the* ***head of the fourth*** *month…etc.* The "head" means the 1st day in each case – *On the first day of the first month*…etc.

Few, if any scholars or priests that I am aware of have considered the texts of Jubilees or Yasher to be the words/laws that the mighty ones of the Eternal One spoke immediately and directly to Moshe on Mt. Horeb prior to leaving for Egypt, but surely, they err in not seeing it. These instructions set up the post Exodus lifestyle we see being depicted in the Exodus stories. Depictions of them *not eating meat or sacrificing animals* in the wilderness, but as it is written – *"and they ate Mannah for 40-years…"* Additionally, as I have proven in my other works, one cannot fall back on Priestly insertions to make the argument from Leviticus or later parts of Exodus, because either the elder texts found in Genesis, Jubilees and early Exodus are correct and true in saying that they murmured and argued with Moshe and God for MEAT while 100,000 head of cattle stood close by, but ate ONLY Mannah for 40 years, or its the later *Priestly* text that make Him and all His subsequent Prophets into liars.

It is clearly understood from the Jubilees, Yasher, Genesis and other texts that these memorial convocations were given and understood to be *Forever* and *Everlasting*. [Which is why they removed the books and or changed certain texts.]

Me'Chudash Zikrone'

מְחֻדָּשׁ זִכְרוֹן

Renewal Memorial

These four Renewal Memorials are all tightly bound together like sheaves of wheat, beginning in heaven with end dates in eternity!

Jub 6:28 *"And on this account,* ***The Eternal ordained these feasts for a memorial forever****, thus are they ordained."*

Each and every year I receive the same questions from both old and new students of this path:

1. How should we observe the 4 Memorials? *And;*
2. How or should we observe the Passover? *And;*
3. Why don't you write a 1st Law Memorial Seder?
   - Everyone on this path should observe the 4 Renewal Memorials as they see fit, and within their own culture and language, and here is why; because, once we are within the Greater Exodus and still keeping these Memorials, how awesome will it be that among millions of *Yehshurim* we have such an amazing and eclectic pool of prayers, foods, and customs to share. Why make it one thing when it can be many things all sharing the same root truth? I get excited just envisioning it.

The main key to answer #1 is, that whatever we do to observe these memorial events, we always do it within the strict confines of the Everlasting Agreement. After that the skies the limit. Or at least technically, the Domes the limit for now.

How or should we observe the Passover?

- Again, this can be a personal preference. Additionally, with the original Exodus event occurring in that same first month I have to consider that the Father timed it exactly to coincide with the *Springtime-mid-month* crops popping out.

Moreover, we have the prophecy of the coming 2nd and Greater Exodus intertwined with that same first Exodus event which has always been the true focal point of that 1st month, 15th-day memorial anyway. And I see no reason to stop anticipating the Greater Exodus.

So again, of course, the 15th-day remembrance memorial event is not the same event *spiritually* as the 4-Renewal Memorials, nor are the two *Ingathering* day events the same. But they are also important. Especially once more of us come together.

Why don't you write a Renewal Memorial Sefer?

- Firstly, for those who may not know, a Memorial "Sefer" or the "Haggadah" is the instructional booklet used to outline a certain holiday event. Order of event, prayers, etc.

The "Jewish" Passover Seder and all the rituals and prayers associated with it have been codified for centuries, and virtually almost all Jews, even Karaites, tend to follow it exactly. This, however, flies in the face of how I just explained how our 4 Renewal Memorials, *Me'Chudash Zikrone'* - should be observed.

Most important, however, and my final answer on this question, is, that if I codified our own specific, *Yehshurim* Haggadah, then THAT would be me codifying a new religion! And I am NOT going to be the one who turns this original and perfect path into yet another vein religion.

LEARN and LIVE the Everlasting Agreement in its time and seasons, your way.

SUMMATION

I know much of this data is new and some may find it difficult to understand certain details, but like with anything new, it takes some time to seep in so don't sweat it. Make a serious attempt to learn the basics so that if need be, in the future you can be used to teach it forward. And consider this, I have already had several people write to me saying that they are worried that they may not be able to find the required constellations when they need to. Again, this comes by SEEING, so do whatever you need to, to be able to find each one in each month and then stare at it to allow your brain to memorize it. Then next time you will just see it.

The basics of this system are for sure the counting of the days between Memorial events – (91) days, but first we MUST have the correct start date, and obviously, the moon phase machine is the best certification of our counting. The moon phases as the world's system currently depict them DO NOT line up correctly in this calendar system because they are all built on this world algorithm, and not His. Which is why we advise physical observations each month.

FYI: Again, our next Spring start date appears to be **March 13th on the Roman calendar**. You can begin your count on that first Renewal Memorial Day to the next 91-day count/seasonal quarter.

To keep it simple for now as you endeavor to learn the 12 required constellations, count the days and then we will use that year's moon phase to confirm that day, on that night.

Other than that I would not sweat it too much.

I would also suggest that everyone, in whatever capacity you may have, in a window, a balcony or a small yard, begin growing some food items. It's good practice, and we cannot hope to be receivers of those stated ingathering day blessings if we are not growing something. Think of it as Greater Exodus practice!

Origin Calendar Pages

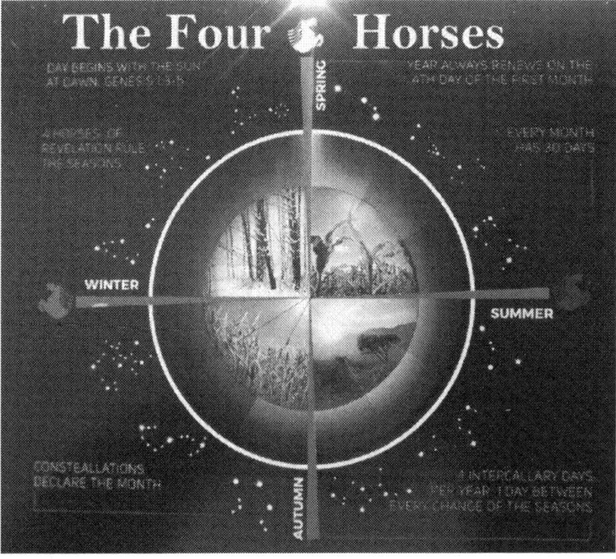

Potasium Phosphate, good as a brain food helpful for nerve and brain imbalances. Foods containing this salt include" "Parsley, Beans, Beets' Carrots, Linseed Meal, Peanuts, Milk Buttermilk, Cheese and Avocados

NAFTALI

"my wrestling"

נפתלי

SEASON CHANGES TO SPRING

DAY 1	DAY 2	DAY 3	DAY 4	DAY 5	DAY 6	DAY 7
		Day of Remembrance [illegible] Passover	1 1st Memorial	2	3	4 SHABBAT
5	6	7	8	9	10	11
12	13	14	15 Exodus GE Lechem day of bread	16	17	18
19	20	21	22	23	24	25
26	27	28	29	30		

Sodium Sulphate, good in regulating the water supply in the body system, decreasing or increasing it as needed. Foods containing this salt include Cauliflower, Lettuce, Cabbage, Turnips, Radishes, Onions, Egg Yolks, Celery, Brussel Sprouts, Kohlrabi, and Milk.

YISSACHAR

"reward"

יששכר

DAY 1	DAY 2	DAY 3	DAY 4	DAY 5	DAY 6	DAY 7
					1	2 SHABBAT
3	4	5	6	7	8	9
10 Watch	11	12	13	14	15	16
17 Watch	18	19	20	21	22	23
24	25	26 Watch	27	28	29	30

Potasium Chloride, good for forming and distributing fiber throughout the body, thereby moderating coagulation. When clogging occurs, it is associated with sinus and throat problems as well as fibrous growths. Foods containing this salt include Cheese, Egg Yolks, Radishes, Coconuts, Lentils.
SHIMEON
"hear"
שמעון
DAY 1
DAY 2
DAY 3
DAY 4
DAY 5
DAY 6
DAY 7
SHABBAT
1
2
3
4
5
6
7
8
9
10
11
12
13
14
15
SHAVU'OT
16
Harvest
60th day
17
18
20
21
22
23
24
25
26
26
28
29
30
Passover
Intercallary Day
SEASON CHANGES TO SUMMER

Calcium Flouride: good for muscle and ligament tonicity (thus helping prevent muscleprolapsis) as well as healthy teeth enamel. Foods containing this salt include: Turnips, Asparagus, Beets, Goat Cheese, Kelp, Garlic, and Pineapple

YOSEF

"added to"

יהוסף

DAY 1	DAY 2	DAY 3	DAY 4	DAY 5	DAY 6	DAY 7
			1. 2nd Memorial Day	2	3	4 SHABBAT
5	6	7	8	9	10	11
12	13	14	15	16	17	18
19	20	21	22	23	24	25
26	27	28	29	30		

Magnesium Phosphate, good for healthy nerve tissue, thus assisting nerve transmission. Foods containing this salt are Cauliflower, Cabbage, Asparagus, Beechnuts, Almonds, Whole Wheat, as well as fruits as Lemons, Limes and Oranges.
YAHUDA
"praise"
יהודה
DAY 1
DAY 2
DAY 3
DAY 4
DAY 5
DAY 6
DAY 7
1 2 3 1 2 1 2
3 4 5 6 7 8 9
10 11 12 13 14 15 16
17 18 19 20 21 22 23
24 25 26 27 28 29 30

Potassium Sulphate, good for circulation of oils through our body which supposedly assists digestion and kidney function, as well as excretion of toxins through the skin. Foods containing this salt include Cauliflower, Lettuce, Cabbage, Onions, Celery, Brussel Sprouts, Tomatoes and Cucumbers.
ASHER
"upright"
אשר
DAY 1
DAY 2
DAY 3
DAY 4
DAY 5
DAY 6
DAY 7
1
2
3
4
5
6
7
8
8/17/17 Sign of Jonah
9
10
11
12
13
14
15
1260th Day of Daniel
16
17
18
19
20
21
22
23
24
25
26
27
28
29
30
Day of Remembrance
Intercallary Day
Pass-Over
SEASON CHANGES TO FALL
1275th Day of Daniel

Sodium Phosphate, good for balancing the acid-alkaline function, helping all acid conditions which affect the nervous system. Foods include: Cottage Cheese, Eggs, Buttermilk, Brown Rice, Tomato Juice, Citrus Fruits & Juices, Whole Wheat products, Lentils, Vegetable Greens and Asparagus.

LEVI

"attached"

אשר

DAY 1	DAY 2	DAY 3	DAY 4	DAY 5	DAY 6	DAY 7
1	2	1	1 3rd Memorial Day	2	3	4
5	6	Noah	8 Daniels	9		11
12	13	14 150 Days	15 1290 Festival of Ingathering	16	17 Ark Rested B4 Sabbath	18
19	20	21	22	23	24	25
26	27	28	29	30		

Calcium Sulphate, good for building and sustaining epithelial tissue; thus supposedly good for all skin diseases. Foods include: Cauliflower, Lettuce, Cabbage, Turnips, Radishes, Onions, Egg Yolks, Celery, Brussel Sprouts, Kohlrabi and Milk

DAN

"judge"

DAY 1	DAY 2	DAY 3	DAY 4	DAY 5	DAY 6	DAY 7
1	2	1	2	1	1	2 SHABBAT
3	4	5	6	7	8	9
10	11	12	13	14	15	16
17	18	19	20	21	22	23
24	25	26	27	28	29	30

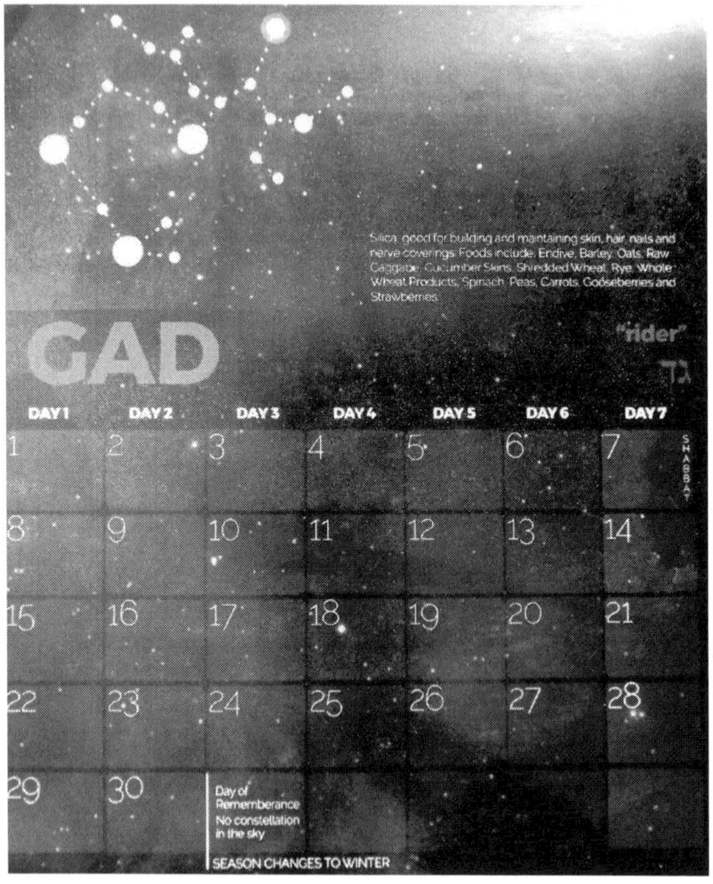
Silica, good for building and maintaining skin, hair, nails and nerve coverings. Foods include: Endive, Barley, Oats, Raw Caggage, Cucumber Skins, Shredded Wheat, Rye, Whole Wheat Products, Spinach, Peas, Carrots, Gooseberries and Strawberries.
GAD
"rider"
גד
DAY 1
DAY 2
DAY 3
DAY 4
DAY 5
DAY 6
DAY 7
SHABBAT
1 2 3 4 5 6 7
8 9 10 11 12 13 14
15 16 17 18 19 20 21
22 23 24 25 26 27 28
29 30
Day of Rememberance
No constellation in the sky
SEASON CHANGES TO WINTER

Calcium Phosphate, good as a bone builder and helpful in any bone disease. Foods include: Parsley, Beans, Beets, Carrots, Linseed Meal, Peanuts, Milk, Buttermilk, Cheese and Avocados

BENYAMIN

"son of the right hand"

בנימין

DAY 1	DAY 2	DAY 3	DAY 4	DAY 5	DAY 6	DAY 7
1	2	3	1 4th Memorial	2	3	4 SHABBAT
5	6	7	8	9	10	11
12	13	14	15	16	17	18
19	20	21	22	23	24	25
26	27	28	29	30		

Sodium Chloride, good for regulating the water supply throughout the body, affecting elimination and how cool or hot we are. Foods include: Onions, Celery, Tomatoes, Almonds, Apples, Spinach, Peaches, Pecans, Lentils, Sauerkraut, Egg Yolks, Swiss Chard, and Coat Cheese.
REUBEN
"see, a son"
ראובן
DAY 1 DAY 2 DAY 3 DAY 4 DAY 5 DAY 6 DAY 7
1 2
SHABBAT
3 4 5 6 7 8 9
End 40days
10 11 12 13 14 15 16
Raven/Dove
17 18 19 20 21 22 23
2nd Dove
Sent out
24 25 26 27 28 29 30
No Dove
Water recedes

Ferrous Phosphate, good for transporting oxygen
throughout the body, aiding circulation, purifying and
of internal organs. Foods include: Raisins, Prunes,
Plums, Grapes, Figs, Oranges, Spinach, Currants,
Mushrooms, Dates, Beets, Wheat Bran and Lima Beans.
WINTER 2018
ZEBULUN
"exalted"
זבלון
DAY 1
DAY 2
DAY 3
DAY 4
DAY 5
DAY 6
DAY 7
1 2 3 4 5 6 7
8 9 10 11 12 13 14
15 16 17 18 19 20 21
22 23 24 25 26 27 28
29 30
Day of Rememberance
Intercalary Day
Pass-Over
SEASON CHANGES TO SPRING

Isaiah 11.11 – *And it will be on that day, the Eternal One will again set His hand, the second time, to recover the remnant of His people that remain from Assyria, and from Egypt, and from Pathros, and from Ethiopia, and from Elam, and from Shinar, and from Hamath, and from the coasts of the sea.* [12] *And He will lift up a banner for the nations, and gather the outcasts of Jacob, and those dispersed from Judah, from the four corners of the earth.*

But only the wise will see and know when!

הושענא אהיה!

Hoshiana Aheeyeh
Save our souls Aheeyeh!

All Asher word translation corrections of all English bible texts herein have been made using the Sephardi transliteration method. Reading these books in the order will provide the student with the clearest and quickest route to understanding many old and long hidden concepts:

1. The Land of Meat & Honey
2. The Greater Exodus
3. Soul Revolution
4. The Beacon Seed
5. The Asher Codex
6. Christendom's False Prophecies

For other topics of extraordinary fair and outside of his standard teachings, join Dr. Asher's AHLCglobal website members area for his weekly Podcasts, radio interviews and also the free blog articles at www.AHLCgobal.com

Why hyper critical Hebrew to English *word*, *grammatical*, and *punctuation* changes are needed when teaching on any biblical subject.

I have answered this question on countless occasions presented by too many people who continue to believe that the Western language bible they have is accurate in every way. Nothing could be further from the truth. However, on this occasion, I thought I might let the reader hear it from another expert on the subject. *S. Asher*

Rabbi B. Barry Levy 1981

Regarding Artscrolls bibles - A large number of grammatical errors exist in their Bible and commentary translations, changing the meaning of these passages.

Dikduk (grammar) is anathema in many Jewish circles, but the translation and presentation of texts are, to a large extent, a philological activity and must be philologically accurate. The ArtScroll effort has not achieved a respectable level. There are dozens of cases where prepositions are misunderstood, where verb tenses are not perceived properly and where grammatical or linguistic terms are used incorrectly. Words are often vocalized incorrectly. These observations, it should be stressed, are not limited to the Bible text but refer to the *Talmudic, Midrashic, targumic,* medieval and modern works as well. Rabbinical passages are removed from their contexts, presented in fragmentary form thus distorting their contents, amended to update their messages even though these new ideas were not expressed in the texts themselves, mis-vocalized, and mistranslated: i.e. misrepresented

The commentary of *Rashbam* to the first chapter of Genesis in ArtScroll's Czuker Edition Hebrew Chumash Mikra'os Gedolos Sefer Bereishis - (2014) has been censored. The missing passages are related to Rashbam's interpretation of the phrase in Genesis 1:5, *"and there was an evening, and there was a morning, one day."* The Talmud cites these words to support the halakhic view that the day begins at sundown. However, Rashbam takes a *peshat* (plain sense) approach, as he does throughout his commentary, reading the verse as follows: *"There was an evening* (at the conclusion of daytime) *and a morning* (at the end of night*), one day";* that is, the day begins in the morning and lasts until the next daybreak. In their defense, ArtScroll points out that in standard Mikra'os Gedolos the entire commentary of Rashbam on the beginning of Bereishis is missing. When adding in from older manuscripts, they left out the exegeses to Genesis 1:5 because of questions about its authenticity, particularly those raised by *Ibn Ezra* in his Iggeres HaShabbos (Letter on Sabbath) who wrote: "heretics put it forth". End quote – (Emphasis added)

So, you see, very few if any lay people who did not grow up in the language and culture can ever delve deep enough, and correctly enough in order to present the entirety of most Hebraic ideas, much less teach an unadulterated truth.

Add to that all of the ongoing malevolent edits to the texts meant to hide original precepts to maintain their control on authority, and it is nothing short of a miracle anyone understands any original truth at all.

About the Author

Dr. Asher is a Hebrew Scholar who emphasizes the absolute, unapologetic distillation of all ancient data regardless of where it leads, or how much it hurts. His most recent work; *"Soul Revolution"* is a magnum opus queued up to eviscerate a plethora of ancient to modern superstitions and religious beliefs via in-depth correlations with ancient texts, prophecies, philosophy, and modern sciences. His latest book – *The Beacon Seed,* is meant to close the circle on the previous hidden original Torah precepts that he has re-unfolded to a quickly expanding population of seekers.

Although surpassing his original Karaite roots, Dr. Asher hails from an uninterrupted family lineage of Torah scholars originating in the Galilee area of Northern Canaan. Dr. Asher's teachings advance the original ancient Karaite philosophy of uncompromising Torah truth based on original Hebrew culture, traditions, and language while disregarding dogmatic religion and superstitions.

Dr. Asher spent most of his childhood in NY & NJ, continuing his learning in his early twenties in Israel where he became a citizen. During his formative years, Dr. Asher was exposed to the Christian religion extensively by those around him. Learning the Torah from the age of seven, he later quickly identified that most *Judeo-Christians* are deeply misinformed on all levels of Hebrew history, culture, ritual, and experience, and thus needed help. Understanding this from a youth, and knowing that it was the duty of all Hebrews - as mandated by the Eternal Creator - to become learned in His *'original Torah'*, apply it to their lives as a light to those around them, and then teach it to all who came in; he left no chance or circumstance to teach anyone who would listen.

In doing so Dr. Asher has dedicated himself to the teaching of the Eternal One's original law to all who wish to leave the worlds false religions and RETURN to the Creator's original path and truth which all souls originally left.

To that end, Dr. Asher formed the Ancient Hebrew Learning Center which has been the focal point for his online instruction. Those who glean insight from Dr. Asher include people from all religious faiths and social status. All of whom are people searching beyond fundamental religions for the more original truth which eludes them. His factual and hard-hitting teachings have been at times controversial because they have been lost for so long, yet enlightening and freeing to all who have embraced them.

Coming Works by Dr. Asher

The ben'Asher Torah
A literal and highly corrected translation of the Torah books known to be attributed directly to Moshe.

Midian to New Egypt
A fact-based fictional story depicting how the Hebrews and mixed multitudes of people leaving Egypt truly lived, rebelled and were split between Mt. Horeb and Mt. Sinai; their religious and cultural separation into two peoples, and their advancements and influences into our modern times.

No Power in the Verse Can Stop Me!

S. Asher

NOTES

Manufactured by Amazon.ca
Bolton, ON